How do

Key Words ... parallel series, each contain... ...ree series are written using the same carefully c... ...led vocabulary. Readers will get the most out of **Key Words** with Peter and Jane when they follow the books in the pattern 1a, 1b, 1c; 2a, 2b, 2c and so on.

• Series a
gradually introduces and repeats new words.

• Series b
provides further practice of these same words, but in a different context and with different illustrations.

• Series c
uses familiar words to teach **phonics** in a methodical way, enabling children to read increasingly difficult words. It also provides a link to writing.

Published by Ladybird Books Ltd
A Penguin Company
Penguin Books Ltd., 80 Strand, London WC2R 0RL, UK
Penguin Books Australia Ltd., Camberwell, Victoria, Australia
Penguin Group (NZ) 67 Apollo Drive, Rosedale, North Shore 0632, New Zealand

009 - 10 9

ISBN: 978-1-40930-122-6

Printed in China

Key Words

with Peter and Jane

5b   Out in the sun

written by W. Murray
illustrated by M. Aitchison

Peter is in bed. Mum comes in to make him get up.

"Come on," she says, "please get up, Peter."

She looks out of the window.

"The sun is out, and there's no school," she says. "You will want to go out in the sun."

Peter jumps out of bed. "Good," he says. "No school and the sun is out."

He looks out of the window. "I see Pat and Dad down there," he says. "They're out in the sun."

"Is Jane up, Mum?" says Peter.

"No, she's not," says Mum. "I'll go and get her up."

new words
out of window sun

Jane is in bed.
Mum comes in to make her get up.

"Come on," she says. "Get up, please, Jane. Peter and Dad are up, and the sun is out."

Jane gets out of bed.

She looks out of the window. "I can see Peter and the dog down there," she says.

Peter looks up at the window. He sees his sister.

"Come on down, Jane," he says. "We're all up. It's good to be out in the sun. We must go out soon."

"Yes," says his sister, "I'll be down soon. I must help Mum and then come down."

new words
sister   must   soon

7

The brother and sister are out at play with some other children. They all like to be out in the sun.

One of the other children has a big red ball. Some of the boys and girls play a game with it.

Then one of the other children makes the ball go into the water.

"We must have a boat to get the ball," says Peter. "Let's ask the man with the boats to help us."

They go to the man with the boats and ask him to help. He says that he will help.

9

The man in the boat will help the children to get the ball out of the water.

Peter gets into the boat with the man.

"Here they come," says Jane to the other children. "Here's the man, and here's my brother. They'll get the ball for us."

As the boat comes to the ball, the man asks Peter to get it.

new word
As as

Peter gets the ball and gives it to the other children. They thank Peter as they go away with the ball. They want to go on with the game.

Peter likes it on the water. He likes to help the man with his boats.

The children are in the water. They like to play in the water in the sun.

Some of them play with a ball in the water. Others sit in the sun.

Jane likes to jump into the water. She jumps in, gets out, and then jumps in again.

"That was good fun," she says.

new words
them   sit
again   going

"Look at me," says Peter. "Look at me up here. See me go down."

Jane looks up as her brother is going down into the water.

"I like that," he says. "See me do it again."

Soon Peter is going down into the water again.

"I must do that," says his sister.

It is the afternoon. The sun is out again this afternoon, and the brother and sister are going for a walk.

They are going to walk up the hill. A boy and girl they know have a house up there.

They want to play with this boy and girl and to have tea with them.

The children stop at a shop to get sweets. They have some of the sweets and they keep some for the boy and girl they are going to see.

They look in the shops as they walk. "Let's look in this shop," says Peter to Jane. "Here are some fish and some rabbits."

new words
afternoon walk
hill know

new words
street by

As they walk down the street the children go by other shops. They like to look in the windows of all the toy shops and sweet shops in the street.

They see other children they know as they walk by the houses.

Soon they come to the station and go in to see the trains.

Then they come out of the station and go on. In the street they see some of the Police. There is one in a Police car.

Peter and Jane can read POLICE on the car. They like to read as they walk down the street. They read STOP, DANGER, STATION and TEAS.

Peter and Jane go by the farm as they walk up the hill. They see a man they know as they go by the farm. He gives them some apples to eat, and asks where they are going.

They thank the man for the apples and sit down to talk to him. Peter eats an apple as they talk.

"We're going up the hill to see a boy and girl we know," says Jane.

"We must be there soon," says Peter, "as we're going to have tea with them."

"Do you know where the house is?" asks the man.

"Yes," says Jane, "we know where it is."

19

The man from the farm and the two children sit in the afternoon sun and talk. The man talks about his work on the farm.

Then Peter says, "We must be off."

"Yes," says the man, "and I must do some work."

As they walk on they see cows, horses and pigs. They stop to see the little pigs run about. "I like to see the little pigs run about in the sun like that," says Jane.

Then they go on up the hill. "We'll soon be there," says Peter. "I can see the house."

The boy and the girl they know are by the house.

new words
from   about   pigs   run

The children talk about where they want to go and what they want to do.

The girls want to get some flowers. The boys want to make boats. Then they want to put them on the water.

The two boys get some things to make the boats. Peter draws his boat. "I want to make it like this," he says.

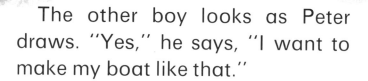

The other boy looks as Peter draws. "Yes," he says, "I want to make my boat like that."

The girls go off up the hill. "We'll see you at tea," they say to the boys.

The boys make the boats and go off to put them on the water.

Here are the two girls. They have some flowers to take home.

"Mum likes flowers," says Jane.

"Yes, my mum likes me to take flowers home," says the other girl.

They walk on the top of the hill. "I like it up here," says Jane.

new words
take top

"Yes," says the other girl, "we all like it up here at the top of the hill. You can see the sea from the top. Look out there."

Jane looks. She can see the sea. "It makes me want to go there," she says.

Soon the girls go down the hill with the flowers. They are going home to help with the tea.

The two boys walk down to the water, with the boats.

Peter puts his boat on the water.

Then the other boy puts his boat on the water. They like this game. It is fun.

The two boys look at the boats as they go by.

new words
now so

"There they go, now," says Peter. "Come on," he says. "We'll go with them. We'll run. Run with me now."

Peter runs, and the other boy runs. They run by the water as they look at the boats.

They don't go into the water, so there is no danger.

"I like this game," says Peter.

"So do I," says the other boy.

It is the afternoon. The sun is out.
The two boys are at play in the sun.
They talk about the boats as they
look down at the water.

"Here come our boats now," says
Peter.

"Yes, here come the two boats,"
says the other boy.

They look down as the boats go
by.

"We must run after our boats
again," says Peter. "Come on, let's
run after them now."

They run off again, by the water.

"We must get our boats out of the water now, so that we can take them home with us," says Peter. "Then we can play with them again."

"How can we get the boats out of the water?" asks Peter.

"I know how we can get them," says the other boy. "We can go into the water here. There's no danger."

The two boys go into the water to get the boats.

They take the boats out of the water, and then come out.

"We can play with the boats again," says Peter.

"Yes," says the other boy, "but now we must go home for tea. The girls will be home by now."

The two boys want some tea. They go home and take the boats with them.

new words
How how but

Here they are again. The children are going to have tea. They are not in the house. They like to eat out in the sun, by a tree. There are no chairs.

"It's fun out here," says Jane. She has some milk, and then she talks to the boys about the walk to the top of the hill.

"We saw the sea," she says.

"Yes," says the other girl, "we saw the sea, and we saw the farm."

The boys eat cake, and talk about the fun they had with the boats and the water.

"We had to go into the water to get our boats out," says Peter.

new words
chairs
saw   had

33

"Come to the house and see my dad draw," says the other girl to Jane.

They go to the house and go to see her dad at work. He sits on a chair as he works. A cat is on the other chair.

As the girl's dad draws he talks to them. "Have you had some fun?" he asks.

They talk to him about the walk they had, and the things they saw.

new word
bag

"Now Jane and I are going for a walk with the boys," says the girl to her dad.

They go down with the boys. The boys have a bag to take with them.

There are apples in the bag.

The children walk by the trees and the water. The girls look at the flowers as they go by. The boys look for rabbits and fish.

Then Peter says, "Look down there. Can you see some men?"

The other children look down. They can see men at work.

"I can see two men," says Jane.

"There are more," says Peter. "I can see more. Let's go down to see what they do."

The boys and girls go on down the hill. They come to where the men work, and sit down to look at them.

The men have a fire. "The fire is for them to make tea," says Peter.

new words
men   more

37

Peter looks in his bag and then they all have an apple. They eat the apples as they look at the men.

There is no danger where they sit.

They talk about the men and the work.

"They are big men," says Peter. "You must be big to do work like that. I want to be big like that."

DANGER
MEN AT
WORK

"Yes, I want to be a big man," says the other boy.

"I don't want to be so big," says his sister.

"I can read what it says there," says Jane. "It says DANGER, MEN AT WORK."

"We can all read it," says her brother.

The boys and girls go on down the hill. As they walk they soon come to the farm again.

One of them sees the dog at work with the man from the farm.

"Let's look at the dog at work," he says.

The children all stop to look.

"I know that man," says Peter.

"Yes, and we know the dog," says Jane. "He's a good dog. He likes children."

The man can make the dog do what he wants. He can make him run or walk, or stop.

Now he makes him sit down.

"The dog likes the work," says Peter. "You can see that."

The man with the dog talks to Peter and Jane.

"Where are the other children?" he asks.

"They said they had to go home," says Peter. "They come from the house on the hill. They're going there now."

The man from the farm talks about his dog, and about the work he can do.

The dog pulls at Jane. "He wants to play now," says Peter.

Jane plays with the dog. The dog pulls Jane, and Jane pulls the dog.

"He likes to work and he likes to play," says the man.

"Come on," he says to the dog. "Stop the game. We have more work to do now."

new words
said pulls

The two children are going home now. They come to the water.

"We have to jump this," says Peter. "Come after me. I know how to do it. Come after me, but keep out of the water."

Jane says, "Mum said that we must keep out of the water."

"I know she said so," says Peter. "I know how to do this now."

Peter jumps again. "You can do it, Jane," he says.

Then Jane jumps. She says, "Yes, I can do it. Look at me, Peter. I can do it."

The children go on. Soon they will come to the street where they can get a bus.

Peter and Jane are in the street. They don't want to walk, so they are going on the bus.

"Which is our bus?" asks Jane. "Which is the one we take?"

"I know which one," Peter says to his sister. "Come with me."

They get on the bus. "Let's go up on top," says Jane. "Then we can see more."

new words
which who

They look out of the window as they go up the street.

"I can see some boys who go to our school," says Peter.

"I can see a girl I know," says Jane. "She has a big dog, and it wants to pull her into a shop."

The children walk home from the bus stop. They want to get home now.

"Mum said that we must come home as the sun is going down," says Jane.

"The sun is going down now," says Peter. "See how red it is. I like to see it like that."

"So do I," says his sister.

"We must go for that walk again," says Peter. "I like to go by the farm and to see the horses and the farm dog."

"Yes, and it's fun to see the little pigs run about up there," says Jane.

Then Peter says, "I can see our house. It will be good to get home."

The brother and sister are at home. They talk to Mum and Dad.

Peter says, "We had fun with our two boats. Then we saw some men at work."

Jane says, "We all had our tea by a tree. Then we saw the man from the farm with his dog."

"You must have had a good afternoon out in the sun," says Mum.

"Yes," says Dad, "but now I know a boy who wants to go to bed."

"Who?" asks Peter.

"You know who," says Dad.

"Yes," says Mum, "and I know a girl who wants to go to bed. Come on, you two. Up to bed you go."

51

New words used in this book

Total number of new words: 46
Average repetition per word: 15